Prices, Poverty, and Inequality

Prices, Poverty, and Inequality

Why Americans Are Better Off Than You Think

Christian Broda and
David E. Weinstein

The AEI Press

Publisher for the American Enterprise Institute

WASHINGTON, D.C.

Distributed to the Trade by National Book Network, 15200 NBN Way, Blue Ridge Summit, PA 17214. To order call toll free 1-800-462-6420 or 1-717-794-3800. For all other inquiries please contact the AEI Press, 1150 Seventeenth Street, N.W., Washington, D.C. 20036 or call 1-800-862-5801.

Library of Congress Cataloging-in-Publication Data

Broda, Christian M. (Christian Miguel), 1975–
  Prices, poverty, and inequality : why Americans are better off than you think / Christian Broda and David E. Weinstein.
    p. cm.
  Includes bibliographical references.
  ISBN-13: 978-0-8447-4275-5
  ISBN-10: 0-8447-4275-9
  1. Poverty—United States. 2. Prices—United States. 3. United States—Economic conditions—1981–2001. 4. United States—Economic conditions—2001–5. Equality—United States. 6. Poor—United States. I. Weinstein, David E. II. Title.

    HC110.P6B75 2008
    339.4'60973—dc22

                                                      2008040991
12 11 10 09 08   1 2 3 4 5

Printed in the United States of America

Contents

List of Illustrations

Introduction

Conventional wisdom holds that economic well-being has stagnated or declined for virtually all Americans over the past twenty-five years except those at the very top of the income distribution. This wisdom takes the form of two commonly held beliefs: that the middle class and the poor are, at best, no better off economically than they were in the early 1980s, and that economic inequality has dramatically increased because those at the top of the income pyramid have captured all of the last three decades' economic gains.

The stagnation of the real wages of poor Americans has been documented in a wide range of sources. For example, the Congressional Budget Office (CBO) estimates that between 1979 and 2005 the real hourly wages of workers at the 10th percentile of the wage distribution rose by only 0.2 percent.[1] Moreover, official nationwide poverty rates have remained essentially unchanged from the 1970s, at around 12 percent of all households. Much of the debate on why incomes have not risen faster for this group of workers has focused on factors related to the workers themselves, such as education and training.

Although these forces are clearly important, relatively little attention has been paid to how nominal wages are converted into real wages in official statistics. In particular, the analysis underlying the common wisdom has tended to assume that the standard official measures of inflation correctly capture the changes in the cost of living of Americans over time, and hence the failure of wages to keep up with prices has been used as prima facie evidence that the poor in America have not benefited from the last several decades of economic growth.

In this monograph we challenge this conventional wisdom by arguing that the price index underlying standard measures of real income ignores two important sources of prosperity for American households: it fails to correctly measure the impact that new and better goods have on Americans' well-being, and it ignores the ability of consumers to substitute away from goods that suddenly become more expensive. First, the consumer price index for all urban consumers (CPI-U for short) almost completely ignores important increases in the quality of existing goods and the increased choice provided by the introduction of new goods. That is, although new household appliances, airbags, new medicines, personal computers, and many other new products and product improvements have benefited the poor over the last few decades, they are only partially captured in current official price statistics. Second, the CPI-U does not account for the behavior of consumers that substitute lower-priced for higher-priced goods when prices change. In fact, once we take these two additional sources of prosperity into account, we find that middle-class and poor Americans have significantly *increased* their economic well-being over the past quarter century. The effects are so dramatic that correctly measured poverty rates have fallen to almost 4 percent of all households over this period.

The reason for the large differences between the standard measures and ours is simple. Product innovation has been a key source of prosperity for American households in recent decades. New and better household appliances, cellular phones, automobile airbags, new medicines, and computers are among the many product improvements that have benefited all Americans, including the poor, during this period. However, current official price statistics only partially capture the benefits of these new and improved goods. Moreover, until changes were made in 1999, the formulas used in the official price index that underlie the poverty statistics systematically understated the well-being of the poor. As we discuss below, this bias arises because the official index ignores the ability of poor consumers to switch their consumption toward goods whose prices are reduced.

Although it is, of course, difficult to measure changes in well-being when the set of goods purchased by households is constantly changing, a large body of empirical and theoretical research has made such measurement feasible. Using this body of work, our analysis focuses on how to extend the version of the CPI-U used to calculate standard measures of poverty to take these sources of prosperity into account. In particular, we show that over the last three decades the true cost of living for Americans has increased by around 1 percentage point per year *less* than what is implied by the CPI-U. This means that many of today's poor are better off than poor people were several decades ago. Over the past few decades, poor households have benefited from the introduction of goods, such as color televisions and microwave ovens, that would have been unaffordable luxuries in the 1960s when the original poverty thresholds were devised.[2]

In a series of papers, we have argued that globalization has played an important role in the increase in new products available to U.S. consumers.[3] Trade with other nations allows U.S. consumers to choose from a variety of goods that are not available to them from domestic producers. For example, it is principally through trade that Americans can purchase Japanese cars, Brazilian coffee, and Irish beer. However, the improvement in consumer welfare achieved through increased variety has tended to go unmeasured: in most economic statistics, coffee is coffee and beer is beer. We have argued that by ignoring the increased choice that international trade provides, economists have underestimated the gains from globalization for the United States. We estimate that globalization has raised the real incomes of Americans, rich and poor alike, and that this effect accounts for around 10 percent of the measured rise in the real wages of the poor.

The reductions in cost-of-living indexes discussed up to now affect all households in America, and so measures of inequality are to a first approximation unaffected by these corrections. However, we also document that the baskets of goods consumed by the rich and the poor differ in ways that are relevant for examining inequality trends. We find two interesting effects. First, over the period 1994–2003, rich households paid around 5 percent more than poor households for identical goods. This effect is typically ignored by conventional measures that assume that the poor and the rich pay the same prices for the goods they both consume. Obviously, some of the difference in the prices paid by wealthy people may reflect nicer "shopping experiences" (for example, in boutiques as opposed to outlet malls) or less time spent shopping. But an important part of the difference arises from truly lower prices in the places where poor people shop. Any such price differential translates into higher real wages for the poor: if the poor pay 5 percent less for identical goods than do the rich, they have 5 percent more real income relative to the rich than national statistics suggest.

Finally, we assess the impact of Chinese imports on American inequality. Interestingly, we find that the U.S. retail sectors where China had the largest increase in market share between 1994 and 2003 are the sectors where retail prices have fallen the most. This is relevant for measures of inequality, since a larger share of the budgets of poor households than of rich households is spent on Chinese imports. Intuitively, the importance of Chinese products is greatest among low-quality products, which make up a larger share of the consumption of poor households. On average over this period, trade with China drove down the prices of retail goods paid by poor families by more than it drove down the prices paid by wealthy households.[4]

The remainder of this monograph is structured as follows. In chapter 1 we review some of the basic economics related to the measurement of prices; we also give examples of the biases in price measurement and summarize their aggregate impact on the CPI-U. In chapter 2 we discuss the impact that CPI biases have on the measurement of poverty rates and the real wages of the poor. In chapter 3 we address differences in composition of the baskets of goods purchased by different income groups and the impact of those differences on inequality. In the last section we present some concluding remarks.

1

Explaining CPI Biases

At the center of our examination of conventional measures of poverty and of the real wages of poor households is the measurement of the true cost of living of Americans. Here we briefly explain why we believe that the CPI-U has drifted away from a true cost-of-living index (COLI) over the last few decades. Specifically, we explain the reasoning behind the claim that substitution and quality biases are inherent in "fixed-goods" price indexes like the CPI-U.

Constructing a COLI involves obtaining information on all the products and services sold in an economy and then aggregating it into a single measure of price changes. This raises a number of analytical and practical problems. Even the most sophisticated statistical office will find it hard to keep up with all product and price developments in a rapidly changing economy. The relative prices of different products change frequently, leading consumers to change their buying patterns. New products are being introduced all the time, and existing ones improved, while others leave the market. There are literally millions of distinct goods and services available in the United States. And as nations become richer, they shift their consumption to goods and services of higher quality and more variety, and (in relative terms) from goods to services. These changes imply that what is consumed today is harder to measure than what was consumed decades ago.

The procedure of aggregating prices is complex. Despite decades of research on the topic, statistical agencies around the world still primarily rely on formulas that do not capture some key aspects of today's dynamic economies. The U.S. CPI, for example, measures the current cost of a fixed basket of goods and services.[1] By contrast, a true COLI would measure the cost of maintaining a certain stand-ard of living, without restrictions on what is in the basket. Although the true cost of living is a recognized measurement goal of the CPI, it is in fact a theoretical construct, not translatable into any single or straightforward index formula that can be used in practice. There-fore it is difficult for the CPI to keep track of all the factors that affect the cost of living. In particular, the continual introduction of new goods in the economy and the changes in relative prices of existing goods create a gap between the CPI-U and a true COLI.

Substitution Bias in the CPI-U

In constructing the CPI-U, the Bureau of Labor Statistics (BLS) selects an array of products whose prices are to be measured and weights these products according to their shares in the consumption of a typical household. These weights, however, remain fixed over time, and so the CPI-U tends to overstate increases in the cost of liv-ing, because it ignores the substitutions among goods that con-sumers make in response to changes in relative prices. For instance, if the price of apples rises relative to that of bananas, consumers will purchase fewer apples and more bananas. Since a fixed-weight index constructed before the price change will now assign a rela-tively larger share to apples (the product whose price has risen) than consumers do, the CPI-U will overestimate the increase in con-sumers' cost of living.[2]

In January 1999 the BLS implemented measures to correct for the substitution that occurs *within* expenditure categories. These adjustments correct for the fact that consumers can, for example, substitute a cheaper type or brand of milk when the price of another type or brand rises. It is believed that most of this "within" or lower-level substitution bias in the CPI-U has been corrected. However, the CPI-U before 1999 still contains this substitution bias, estimated conservatively at between 0.1 and 0.2 percentage point per year. Substitution may also occur *across* the CPI's roughly 300 expendi-ture categories, for example buying more tea when the price of coffee rises. One can easily obtain an estimate of the resulting

TABLE 1-1
UPPER-LEVEL SUBSTITUTION BIAS:
THE IMPACT OF CHAINING IN U.S. CPI INFLATION

	CPI	C-CPI	Average inflation difference
2001	2.8%	2.3%	0.6%
2002	1.6%	1.2%	0.3%
2003	2.3%	2.1%	0.2%
2004	2.7%	2.5%	0.2%
2005	3.4%	2.9%	0.5%
2006	3.2%	2.8%	0.4%
Average			0.4%

Source: U.S. Bureau of Labor Statistics.

upper-level substitution bias by comparing the CPI-U with a measure of prices that takes this substitution into account, such as the C-CPI-U, which is a chained price index. Such an index reweights the consumption basket according to actual consumption patterns each year and uses mathematical formulas to "chain" the annual index values together in an appropriate way. New evidence by Lebow and Rudd (2003) suggests that this bias was around 0.5 percentage point per year in 1998–2000. Table 1-1 extends their comparison to the present to show that this bias has been roughly 0.4 percentage point per year for the period since 2000. For future reference we assume a conservative estimate for the *total* substitution bias in past decades of 0.4 percentage point per year.

New Goods and Quality Bias in the CPI-U

The second main deviation of the CPI-U from a true COLI that concerns us here comes from the new products that are constantly being introduced into the marketplace. Some of these are similar to existing products, but many have improved our standard of living in significant ways. Cellular phones, DVDs, and the personal computer are just a few familiar examples. The introduction of these new goods should reduce the cost of maintaining a given level of consumer well-being (or increase well-being for a given cost), but this is not appropriately captured in current official measures.[3] In the next two subsections we illustrate the impact that increased variety and higher quality have on the measurement of prices, on the basis of two recent studies.[4]

Product Turnover and Quality Upgrades. The Advisory Commission to Study the Consumer Price Index (1996; also known as the Boskin Commission after its chairman, Michael Boskin) used findings from a few previous studies that had estimated quality biases in specific product sectors and extrapolated these to the entire CPI. On this basis the commission argued that the overall quality bias in the CPI-U was around 0.6 percentage point per year. In a recent survey Lebow and Rudd (2003) discuss the improvements in price measurement made in response to the Boskin Commission's recommendations and conclude that the estimates of quality bias in sectors accounting for less than 10 percent of the CPI were based on "at least a moderate degree of hard evidence" (163). The rest were either based on inadequate evidence or entirely subjective. In a recent paper (Broda and Weinstein 2008) we try to address this shortcoming in the calculation of the aggregate quality bias. We use extremely detailed price and quantity data at the barcode level to estimate changes in quality and all the other parameters necessary to compute an exact *aggregate* price index for almost half of the goods in the CPI.

To explore these effects we use a new data set that only recently has become available for research. The ACNielsen Homescan database provides information on every purchase of a good with a Universal Product Code (UPC) by a representative sample of approximately 55,000 households. This database covers mainly products sold in grocery, drugstores, and mass-merchandise stores, which account for close to 40 percent of all expenditure on goods in the CPI. In a typical quarter the database lets us observe prices and quantities purchased of approximately 700,000 goods. By contrast, the BLS uses a sample that is only about 5 percent as large when it computes prices for these sectors. A second important feature of our data is that we observe all actual purchases of households, so that we can detect when a good is purchased for the first time or when it ceases to be sold. By contrast, the CPI is based on a sample of goods that remains unchanged over a four- to five-year period. Thus it typically does not incorporate new goods when they appear, but only after they have been in the market for a number of years.[5]

To illustrate the impact of new goods for consumers, consider the following thought experiment. Before a new good is introduced, demand for it is effectively zero, the same as if it were already on the market but at a prohibitively high price. Its introduction thus affects the consumer in the same way as if the good's price had just declined from the prohibitively high "reservation" price to the observed price. Similarly, a product exiting the market can be seen as one whose price has increased from the market price to its reservation price. Since new and disappearing goods are not included in the CPI, the index does not include goods whose prices move to and from their reservation price.[6]

Davis and Haltiwanger (1992) use the reservation price concept to provide a means of assessing the severity of the problem of ignoring product entry and exit in constructing price indexes. Let p_{ut} be the price of a given product u with a unique UPC at time t; then the mean growth rate g of that good's price can be defined as

1) $$g_{ut} = \frac{P_{ut} - P_{ut-1}}{\frac{1}{2}(P_{ut} + P_{ut-1})}$$

The mean growth rate is a simple transformation of the conventional growth rate.[7] The major difference between the two growth rates is that by assuming a specific reservation price for the new and exiting products, we can represent price changes for all products using this statistic. For expositional ease, we assume for the time being that the reservation price is infinite for goods that appear or disappear. This

FIGURE 1-1

DISTRIBUTION OF PRICE CHANGES BY
UNIVERSAL PRODUCT CODE, 1999–2003

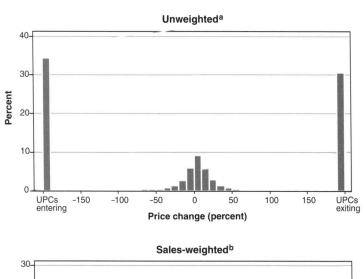

Unweighted[a]

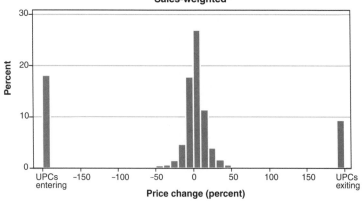

Sales-weighted[b]

SOURCE: ACNielsen Homescan.
NOTES: a. Each observation represents the change in price of a single UPC; b. each observation is weighted by its share of sales of all goods.

implies that the mean growth rate is confined to the range of –2 (at product u's introduction) to 2 (at its exit from the market).

Figure 1-1 plots the distribution of price growth rates thus defined for all goods in our sample over the period 1999–2003. Over this five-year period, products whose prices moved to or from their reservation price (exited or entered) account for over 60 percent of the number of goods in the sample (top panel). Clearly any price index based only on a common set of goods available over an entire period is thus likely to be problematic, because it ignores a sizable number of goods whose prices are undergoing large changes. In the bottom panel, in which products are weighted by sales, the entry and exit of products is again an unmistakable feature of the distribution: over 25 percent of the goods (in average sales-weighted terms) either were introduced or disappeared during the period. Since the weight used to scale this figure is an average taken over both t and t–1, new and exiting goods always have a weight equal to zero at one point in time. Thus their importance at any one time where they are available is roughly twice as large. In other words, these same data imply that 37 percent of expenditure in 2003 was on goods that did not exist in 1999, and 18 percent of expenditure in 1999 was on goods that did not survive until 2003. Moreover, to the extent that the value of goods created over the period exceeds the value of goods that disappeared, a greater share of goods experiences unobserved price declines than unobserved price increases. This fact is important, because it establishes that the mean of the full distribution lies to the left of the mean of the distribution of price changes of goods available throughout the period. In other words, a price index that does not take product birth and death into account is likely to be biased upward.

Table 1-2 summarizes the extent of product creation and destruction using weighted and unweighted measures at different frequencies. The first column presents data on entry and exit between 1994 and 2003, and the second reports the corresponding numbers between 1999 and 2003. In each case the table reports the following measures of product entry and exit and creation and destruction of value as measured by expenditure on those products:

2)   Entry Rate (t) = $\dfrac{\text{\# New UPCs } (t)}{\text{\# All UPCs } (t)}$;

Exit Rate $(t\text{-}1)$ = $\dfrac{\text{\# Disappearing UPCs } (t\text{-}1)}{\text{\# All UPCs } (t\text{-}1)}$

Creation (t) = $\dfrac{\text{Value of New UPCs } (t)}{\text{Total Value } (t)}$;

Destruction $(t\text{-}1)$ = $\dfrac{\text{Value of Disappearing UPCs } (t\text{-}1)}{\text{Total Value } (t\text{-}1)}$

Table 1-2 reveals that almost 80 percent of the UPCs that existed in 2003 did not exist in 1994. These new products accounted for 64 percent of expenditure in 2003. Meanwhile 72 percent of all UPCs existing in 1994 had disappeared by 2003, and their value was much smaller—37 percent of expenditure in 1994—than that of the new products in 2003. This suggests that the new UPCs systematically displaced market share from the UPCs that were available throughout this period ("common" UPCs). This can also be summarized in terms of the ratio of the shares of common UPCs. The last row in the table shows that this ratio is below unity: the share of common UPCs was larger in 1994 than in 2003. As we will emphasize below, this is an important indication that the new products are of a higher average quality than the products that exited.

In Broda and Weinstein (2008) we measure the impact of this creative destruction of products on consumer welfare. We show that the fact that the new goods have a larger share in consumption than the disappearing goods reveals that the price per "quality unit" of the entering class of goods is lower than that of the exiting set of goods. This implies that the overall quality of goods available to the consumer is rising, even though a fixed-goods price index, based only on the set of common goods, ignores that rise in quality. When we adjust the CPI-U for these changes in quality, we find that it has been overstating inflation by around 0.8 percentage point per year for the set of goods in our sample. This is actually less than the upward bias of 1.4 percentage point per year that Bils and Klenow

TABLE 1-2
PRODUCT ENTRY AND EXIT BY NUMBER OF PRODUCTS AND BY
EXPENDITURE SHARE, 1994–2003 AND 1999–2003

	1994–2003 (Percent)	1999–2003 (Percent)
Product entry rate[a]	78	50
Creation rate[b]	64	37
Relative size of entering products[c]	49	56
Product exit rate[d]	72	46
Destruction rate[e]	37	18
Relative size of exiting products[f]	23	23
Ratio of shares of common goods at beginning and end of period[g]	57	77

SOURCE: Authors' calculations.
NOTES: a. Number of new products (products with a unique UPC in the sample in 2003 that were not in the sample in the initial year of the period) divided by the total number of products in 2003; b. expenditure on new products divided by total expenditure in 2003; c. average sales of new UPCs relative to the average sales of existing UPCs; d. number of exiting products (products with a unique UPC in the sample in the initial year of the period that were no longer in the sample in 2003) divided by the total number of products in the initial year of the period; e. expenditure on exiting products divided by total expenditure in the initial year of the period; f. average sales of discontinued UPCs relative to the average sales of existing UPCs; g. share of expenditure on all UPCs available in 2003 that are available throughout the period (one minus the creation rate, or 36 percent for 1994–2003) divided by the share of expenditure on all UPCs available in the initial year that are available throughout the period (one minus the destruction rate, or 63 percent for 1994–2003).

(2001) found for durable consumer goods, but it still constitutes an important source of unmeasured increase in the standard of living of American households.

Table 1-3 presents a summary of estimates of the biases that arise from ignoring new and quality-upgraded goods and the possibility of substitution. The bias of 0.8 percentage point per year found by Broda and Weinstein (2008) applies to 23 percent of expenditure in the CPI. This implies an upward bias of 0.18 percentage point per year in the CPI as a whole. Similarly, the 1.4-percentage-point bias for consumer durables found by Bils and Klenow applies to 10 percent

TABLE 1-3
ADDING UP CPI-U BIASES

Source	Bias (percentage points)	Weight in CPI of items affected (percent)	Impact on CPI [a] (percentage points)
Total substitution bias prior to 1999	0.4	100	0.40
Broda and Weinstein (2008)	0.8	23	0.18
Bils and Klenow (2001)[b]	1.4	10	0.14
Nonhousing services[c]	1.1	28	0.31
Housing shelter services[d]	0.0	32	0.00
Total bias			1.03

SOURCE: Literature cited and authors' calculations.
NOTES: a. Product of the first two columns; b. this is two-thirds the number in Bils and Klenow (2001). The other third has been corrected by the use of hedonics; c. bias is assumed to equal the average bias for all goods; d. assumed to be zero.

of consumption and therefore biases the CPI upward by 0.14 percentage point per year. The above estimates measure bias only in goods; similar biases are likely to be present in the services sector, but this is much harder to measure. The reason is that it is often difficult to define precisely what is being consumed in sectors such as education, finance, and entertainment, whereas in goods markets, products can be narrowly defined. A reasonable assumption, however, is that the rate of innovation in nonhousing services is equal to the average rate observed in the goods sectors. Assuming for convenience that no bias exists in the housing services sectors, this means that the overall current bias relating to new goods and improved quality in the CPI-U is around 0.6 percentage point per year. In addition, based on Lebow and Rudd's (2003) findings and table 1-1, we argue that the overall substitution bias is around 0.4 percentage point per year, of which 0.3 percentage point comes from ignoring upper-level substitution.

Summing together the biases from these different sources, we obtain an overall CPI bias of 1.0 percentage point per year. The results that follow are based on this benchmark estimate. Notice that this is a conservative estimate compared with that presented in the work of Costa (2001) and Hamilton (2001). They calculate a CPI bias by estimating the income elasticity of food and recreation, using cross-sectional micro data pooled across all years in which consumer expenditure surveys are available, and using these estimates to measure the increase in households' real income over time, controlling for changes in relative prices and in demographic characteristics. This procedure measures bias attributable to consumer substitution, increases in the durability of goods, the late introduction of new goods into the CPI, changes in the distribution network, and the mismeasurement of prices. Using this alternative method, Costa (2001) finds that the total CPI bias during the period 1972–94 was 1.6 percentage points, over 50 percent larger than our benchmark estimate.

Figure 1-2 compares the paths of different measures of the CPI-U between 1990 and 2005. The top series is the standard CPI-U, and the second is the CPI that would have obtained if the innovations implemented in 1999 had been implemented earlier (this CPI research series, or CPI-U-RS, is calculated by the BLS). The principal difference between the two series arises from the use of geometric averaging at the lower (within-categories) level. After 1999, as one might expect, the two series move in a parallel fashion. The third series from the top makes the adjustment for chaining at the upper (across-categories) level and therefore corrects for the bulk of the substitution bias. For the period since 2001 it uses the official C-CPI-U, and it is extrapolated backward on the assumption that the upper-level substitution bias is around 0.3 percentage point per year. These assumptions imply that over fifteen years, using the official methodology applied since 1999 extrapolated all the way back to 1990, prices have risen by 10 percentage points less than one might surmise from the CPI-U.

The bottom series in the figure is our own adjusted cost-of-living index, the C-CPI-U-BW, which makes, in addition to the adjustment for chaining, an adjustment for new products and quality upgrading.

FIGURE 1-2
ALTERNATIVE CONSUMER PRICE INDEXES, 1990–2005

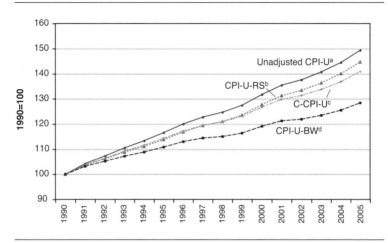

SOURCES: U.S. Bureau of Labor Statistics and authors' calculations.
NOTES: a. CPI for all urban consumers, reindexed from 1982–84 base to 1990; b. CPI-U research series; c. chained CPI-U, extrapolated backward from 2001 by the authors; d. chained CPI constructed by the authors, which adjusts for new product entry and quality upgrading.

As table 1-3 suggests, this bias has been around 0.6 percentage point per year. This series implies that inflation rates were around 1 percentage point per year lower than the CPI-U suggests, and prices 20 percent lower at the end of the period.

Globalization and New Goods. One development that has significantly broadened consumers' choice in recent decades is the growth of international trade. Trade gives consumers the ability to purchase goods they would not otherwise have access to, and it increases the variety of goods in the marketplace. In this section we quantify the gains for U.S. consumers from having access to a wider set of goods available for consumption, and we discuss why they are not captured by the import price index.

This improvement in consumer welfare from increased variety has tended to go unmeasured. If the prices of all varieties of coffee are the same, a conventional price index will not change with the number of types of coffee available. However, consumers in an economy with more varieties will probably consider themselves better off than consumers whose only choice is between Folgers and Maxwell House. The fact that the price index in the higher-variety economy does not capture the greater well-being of consumers relative to the single-variety economy illustrates the nature of the new goods bias. It implies that the extent to which the American consumer is better off due to new and better imported goods is not reflected in the measures of well-being calculated by national statistics.

To examine the role that globalization has played in increasing the number of varieties available to consumers, we first examine the growth of imported varieties in the United States using the most disaggregated import data available for the period between 1972 and 2001.[8] We then examine how much the observed increase in imported varieties has raised U.S. welfare by reducing the true cost of living.

The most disaggregated U.S. trade data available are those in the Tariff Schedule for the United States, Annotated (TSUSA, an eight-digit classification, each digit representing a level of subcategorization) and the Harmonized Schedule (HS, a ten-digit classification). Both data sets break U.S. imports down into approximately 15,000 separate goods, with definitions like "red wine in bottles of under 1 liter." We define a variety to be a good at the lowest classification level exported by a particular country, for example, "French red wine in bottles of under 1 liter." This definition illustrates both the power and the shortcomings of working with trade data. On the one hand, it enables us to examine the interactions of literally hundreds of thousands of varieties—a level of disaggregation so fine that the typical consumer spends an average of no more than a penny per year on each variety. On the other hand, as the example of French red wine indicates, the data still aggregate together many "varieties" in a single subcategory (for example, Bordeaux and Burgundy, to say nothing of the many individual geographic appellations and varietals).[9]

Table 1-4, which reports the change over time in the total number of varieties of goods imported by the United States, reveals an

TABLE 1-4
VARIETY IN U.S. IMPORTS, 1972–2001

Goods sample	Year	No. of TSUSA or HS categories[a]
1972–88		
All goods available in 1972	1972	7,731
All goods available in 1988	1988	12,822
Goods common to 1972–88	1972	4,167
Goods common to 1972–88	1988	4,167
Goods available in 1972 but not in 1988	1972	3,553
Goods available in 1988 but not in 1972	1988	8,640
1990–2001		
All goods available in 1990	1990	14,572
All goods available in 2001	2001	16,390
Goods common to 1990–2001	1990	10,636
Goods common to 1990–2001	2001	10,636
Goods available in 1990 but not in 2001	1990	3,936
Goods available in 2001 but not in 1990	2001	5,754

SOURCE: Robert C. Feenstra, John Romalis, and Peter K. Schott. 2002. "U.S. Imports, Exports, and Tariff Data," Working Paper #9387. Cambridge, Mass: National Bureau of Economic Research. http://cid.econ.ucdavis.edu/usixd/wp5515d.html.

unmistakable trend. This total (far right-hand column) rose 133 percent in the first period and 57 percent in the second. Roughly half of this increase appears to have been driven by an increase in the number of categories, and half by an increase in the median number of countries supplying each good.

To get a more concrete sense of what is driving these movements, it is worthwhile to look at some sample categories. In some cases the growth in varieties arises from a clear increase in the number of countries exporting a given well-defined good. For example, in 1972 the United States imported roasted or ground coffee from twenty-five countries. By 2001, however, the United States was importing roasted coffee from fifty-two countries.[10] Similarly, the

Median no. of exporting countries	Average no. of exporting countries	Total no. of varieties (country-good pairs)
6	9.2	71,420
9	12.2	156,669
6	8.4	35,060
10	12.2	50,969
7	10.2	36,355
8	12.7	105,696
10	12.5	182,375
12	15.8	259,215
10	12.4	132,417
13	16.3	173,776
10	12.7	49,958
11	14.8	85,439

NOTE: a. Categories for 1972–88 are TSUSA categories; those for 1990–2001 are HS categories.

number of countries supplying beer and wine to the United States rose by about 195 percent and 50 percent, respectively. Some non-food items experienced comparable or even larger increases; for example, the number of countries supplying eyeglasses rose from nine to forty-seven.

In other cases the growth involves a mix of new goods and new sources. Car audio is a good example. In 1972 twenty-one countries exported car radios of all types to the United States, all classed in a single category. By 2001 there were nine different categories for car audio systems, with as many as twenty-eight countries exporting each category. In all, the apparent number of varieties rose from 21 to 174. Clearly some of this increase, for example splitting the single 1972 category into the 2001 categories of AM radios and AM/FM radios, does not represent an increase in new goods. Other categories, however, such as radios with tape and CD players, or radios with just CD players, probably do constitute a bona fide increase in choice.

What countries is the increased variety coming from? Table 1-5 ranks countries by the numbers of goods they exported to the United States in four different years. The first column ranks the top twenty countries from highest to lowest for 1972, and the following columns rank the same countries for subsequent years. Not surprisingly, the countries that export the most varieties to the United States tend to be large, high-income economies that are close geographically. Looking at what has happened to the relative rankings over time, however, reveals a number of interesting stylized facts. First, Canada and Mexico have risen sharply in the rankings. Canada moved from being the fourth-largest source of varieties to first place, while Mexico moved from thirteenth to eighth place. This may reflect the creation of the Canada-U.S. Free Trade Area in 1989 and the North American Free Trade Area in 1994.

Economic growth, perhaps coupled with other forms of trade liberalization, also appears to have played some role. Several fast-growing economies such as China (not shown in table 1-5) and South Korea rose dramatically in the rankings. Indeed, the growth of varieties from China is stunning. In 1972 China only exported 710 different goods to the United States, but by 2001 it was exporting 10,315. In other words, whereas Chinese firms competed in only 0.8 percent of U.S. import markets in existence in 1972, by 2001 they participated in 63 percent. Although Chinese firms still account for only 9 percent of all U.S. imports, there is at least one Chinese firm selling in almost two-thirds of U.S. import markets.

The more than thirteen-fold increase in the number of varieties exported by China has produced a dramatic change in China's relative position, from only the twenty-eighth most important source of varieties in 1972 to the fourth most important today. Similarly, after India began its period of liberalization in the last decade, its economic growth rate rose sharply, as did the number of goods it began

TABLE 1-5
RANKING OF COUNTRIES BY NUMBER OF GOODS EXPORTED
TO THE UNITED STATES, 1972, 1988, 1990, AND 2001

Country	Ranking			
	1972	1988	1990	2001
Japan	1	1	3	7
United Kingdom	2	4	4	3
Germany	3	3	2	2
Canada	4	2	1	1
France	5	6	5	6
Italy	6	5	6	5
Switzerland	7	11	11	11
Hong Kong	8	9	12	16
Netherlands	9	13	13	14
Taiwan	10	7	7	9
Spain	11	14	15	12
Belgium and Luxembourg	12	15	14	15
Mexico	13	12	10	8
Sweden	14	17	16	19
Denmark	15	22	21	23
Austria	16	18	18	21
India	17	19	23	13
Rep. of Korea	18	8	9	10
Brazil	19	16	17	18
Australia	20	20	20	20

SOURCE: Feenstra et al. (2002).
NOTE: Table includes only the top twenty countries in 1972. By 2001 China was the fourth largest exporter of varieties.

exporting. At the other extreme are economies like Japan and Argentina, which have seen fairly substantial drops in the number of varieties they export.

As mentioned above, standard national statistics do not account for how much better off consumers are when a new good or a new variety of an existing good becomes available. In particular, the commonly used price indexes measure the current cost of a fixed-weight basket of goods and services.[11] The introduction of new goods in the market increases a country's standard of living and therefore should reduce the cost of maintaining consumer well-being. Thus increases in the variety of goods available for consumption lower a true COLI but are mostly ignored in the way fixed-weight price indexes are currently measured.

Measuring the impact of this increase on U.S. welfare is a complex process. A fundamental input to the calculation of a true COLI that incorporates variety growth is the degree of substitutability between different varieties of a given good. The magnitude of the gain from variety depends on how similar the new varieties are relative to existing varieties of the same good. For example, if Irish beer is not a perfect substitute for American beer, U.S. consumers benefit from trade with Ireland because it enables them to consume both varieties. Obviously, if varieties are highly substitutable, as might be true for varieties of gasoline, for example, then increasing the number of varieties is unlikely to have much of an effect on welfare.

Broda and Weinstein (2006) use Feenstra's (1994) methodology to estimate 30,000 elasticities of substitution between pairs of goods using the same disaggregated trade data discussed above. (The higher the substitution elasticity between two goods, the more willing consumers are to substitute one for the other when their relative price changes.) Not surprisingly, we find that between 1972 and 1988, among sectors with the most imports by value, the highest elasticity of substitution was among varieties of crude petroleum and shale oil. The estimated elasticity of substitution for this sector was 9.7, almost five times the elasticity among varieties of footwear (2.0), the sector with the lowest elasticity in this group. For the same period we also find that sectors related to petroleum have the highest elasticities.

Broda and Weinstein (2006) show that combining increases in the number of varieties with their appropriate degree of substitutability yields a measure of the increase in well-being that new sources of variety provide. We find that when variety growth is accounted for, the true cost of living related to imported goods fell

22.5 percentage points faster than the unadjusted cost between 1972 and 1988, or about 1.6 percent per year. Interestingly, the impact of variety growth was much smaller during the 1990s. Between 1990 and 2001 this growth of varieties meant that the adjusted COLI fell 5 percent faster than the unadjusted index over this period, or about 0.5 percent per year. Over the entire period, we find that the growth of varieties reduces the exact price relative to the conventionally measured import price index by 28.1 percentage points, or 1.2 percentage points per year.

2

CPI Biases and Poverty Measures

Thus far we have been concerned with documenting the importance of new varieties and their implications for price measurement. One of the principal conclusions of this analysis is that prices have been rising less rapidly than is reported in the CPI. We now turn to examining the implications that this has for the measurement of real income. Since all real income measures involve deflating the nominal income of households by a price index, these measures are sensitive to how prices are measured. As we will see in the subsequent sections, this has important implications for our understanding of how real wages have evolved as well as for our measurement of poverty.

Real Wages of the Poor Using Alternative Inflation Measures

Table 2-1 shows the impact of adjusting the nominal wages of U.S. workers at the 10th percentile of the wage distribution with different price indexes. The first row shows the conventional measure of real wages, based on the CPI-U, used by the U.S. Census Bureau and other national statistical offices. In 2005 workers at the 10th percentile earned nominal wages of $7.44 per hour; in 1979 their average hourly wage in 2005 dollars was $7.43. In other words, according to the official statistics, the real wage at this point of the income distribution remained virtually unchanged over this twenty-six-year period. This is the basis for the contention that despite the tremendous growth of the U.S. economy over this period, the gains have not trickled down to the poorest Americans.

However, if we correct for substitution bias in the standard CPI as described above (using the C-CPI-U, third row of table 2-1), we

TABLE 2-1
REAL HOURLY WAGES AT THE 10TH PERCENTILE
USING ALTERNATIVE DEFLATORS, 1979–2005

Deflator	Constant (2005) dollars				
	1979	1990	1994	2000	2005
CPI for all urban consumers (CPI-U)	7.43	6.60	6.54	7.35	7.44
CPI-U research series (CPI-U-RS)	7.07	6.38	6.46	7.34	7.44
Chained CPI-U (C-CPI-U)	6.62	6.10	6.22	7.22	7.44
Authors' adjusted CPI-U (C-CPI-U-BW)	5.70	5.48	5.74	6.97	7.44
Memoranda: Percent change from indicated year to 2005					
CPI for all urban consumers (CPI-U)	0.1	12.7	13.8	1.2	0.0
CPI-U research series (CPI-U-RS)	5.2	16.6	15.1	1.3	0.0
Chained CPI-U (C-CPI-U)	12.5	22.1	19.5	3.0	0.0
Authors' adjusted CPI-U (C-CPI-U-BW)	30.6	35.8	29.6	6.8	0.0

SOURCE: Feenstra et al. (2002) and authors' calculations.

find that wages at the 10th percentile are in fact 13 percent higher today than they were in 1979. This adjustment simply corrects for the fact that poor households can switch their consumption to those categories of goods whose relative price has fallen. Given how well understood the substitution bias is, it is surprising that the public debate still does not acknowledge this increase in the wages of the poor.

If, in addition, we allow for the correction for new and higher-quality products (using our own adjusted measure, the C-CPI-U-BW, fourth row of table 2-1), the real wages at the 10th percentile have increased by fully 30 percent since 1979. In other words, the real wages of these low earners have not remained stagnant, as suggested by conventional measures, but actually have been rising on average by around 1 percent per year. This means that the well-being of the poor is substantially greater today than it was twenty-five years ago.

TABLE 2-2

OWNERSHIP OF SELECTED CONSUMER GOODS
AMONG POOR HOUSEHOLDS

Consumer good	Percent of poor households owning
Air conditioner	79.7
Clothes washer	64.3
Clothes dryer	56.7
Dishwasher	36.5
Microwave oven	88.7
Color television	97.3
VCR or DVD player	78.0
Stereo	58.6
Personal computer	36.0

SOURCE: U.S. Census Bureau, American Housing Survey for the United States 2003 and 2005.

The Impact on Poverty Rates

The impact of these adjusted measures of inflation on poverty rates
in the United States is even more dramatic. Poverty is conventionally defined as living on an income below a certain threshold, called
the poverty line. Different poverty lines are established for households of differing size and were initially set in 1965. The thresholds
are updated by the CPI-U each year but otherwise have undergone
only a few minor modifications. However, as we have documented,
this index is biased upward both for the conventional reasons that
have often been discussed and because the index does not include
the impact of new and better goods.

Table 2-2 provides a sense of the importance of this bias for poor
households. Well over half of all poor households have at least one
microwave oven, color television, and VCR or DVD player, and over
half have cable or satellite TV service. None of these goods existed in
the early 1960s, when the consumption baskets for poor households

were defined. Yet these goods have indisputably increased the well-being of those who own them. Furthermore, many goods have undergone substantial quality improvements over the last forty years, which are not captured by a price index based on a set of common goods.

We can compute the impact that the introduction of new goods and quality improvements in existing goods have had on poverty rates in the United States through the following exercise. Because we do not have estimates of the biases in all of our price indexes going back before the 1990s, we decided to focus on movements in poverty between 1990 and 2006. We use the Public Use Microdata Sample (PUMS) and other census data to compute poverty rates in 1990 for each class of household. First, we update the poverty thresholds using the CPI-U between 1991 and 2006; this gives us the official poverty rates (with a slight difference because the sample of households in the PUMS differs from that on which the official poverty rate estimation is based). Next we recompute the thresholds using the chained CPI (C-CPI-U) and the Broda-Weinstein adjusted index (C-CPI-U-BW). Finally, we extrapolate the differences in the last fifteen years between the official and the adjusted thresholds back to 1970.

Figure 2-1 presents the results from this exercise. The first striking observation is the difference in poverty levels between inflation measures. When the official, unchained CPI-U is used as the deflator, 9.7 percent of all families were in poverty in 2000, rising to 10.7 percent by 2006. But when the chained CPI is used instead, poverty is about 25 percent lower (roughly 2.5 percentage points) in each of these years. If we make the further adjustment of taking into account new goods, poverty rates fall further: when the Broda-Weinstein index is used as the deflator, by 2000 poverty is less than half what it is in the official statistics. In other words, the observed stability of the official poverty rate arises from failing to adjust for the fact that the poor have access to new and better goods.

Extrapolating these results back to 1970 gives some sense of the magnitude of these differences over the long run. Over the past fifteen years, the difference in methodologies for computing inflation

FIGURE 2-1

ALTERNATIVE MEASURES OF THE POVERTY RATE, 1970–2006

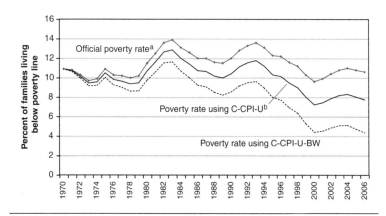

SOURCES: U.S. Census Bureau, Poverty Thresholds, http://www.census.gov/hhes/www/poverty/threshld.html and authors' calculations.

NOTES: a. The official poverty rate uses the CPI-U to deflate prices; b. see figure 1-2 and the text for definitions of the C-CPI-U and the C-CPI-U-BW. Both measures assume constant substitution and quality bias throughout the period. The estimates of the substitution bias are based on the 2000–6 period and those of the quality bias on the 1994–2003 period.

rates has produced a poverty rate that rises by 1.7 percentage points per decade faster than the rate based on the actual bundle of goods consumed. This implies that if the statistical agencies had used a quality-adjusted chained index instead of the CPI-U to adjust the poverty line, the actual poverty rate in 2006 would have fallen by 60 percent since 1970.

3

Prices and Inequality, 1990–2005

Thus far we have been discussing how corrections in price measurement can have important implications for understanding the evolution of real wages and poverty in the United States. However, careful analysis of price indexes can also have important implications for our understanding of the distribution of income. Some recent work has already examined how an awareness of the different consumption patterns of rich and poor households might affect our understanding of income distribution. For example, an increase in the price of restaurant meals is more likely to affect wealthy households than poor ones. However, little analysis has been done of the microstructure of expenditure patterns of rich and poor households.

Obviously, the prices that any household pays for a given good can depend greatly on where the good is purchased and whether the good is on sale. However, here we explore more systematic variations in how wealthier and poorer households make consumption decisions.

How Do Consumption Baskets Differ by Income Level?

We begin by considering "quality Engel curves." These curves describe how the quality of goods purchased by households increases as their income rises. Within almost any "module" or large category of products—say, tobacco and accessories—there are a large number of individual UPCs. By regressing the unit prices of households' purchases of each of these UPCs on household expenditure per adult, we can see whether wealthier households tend to spend more on certain varieties of UPCs rather than others within the same module. Results from such a regression for 128 product groups (table 3-1) indicate

TABLE 3-1
ESTIMATED QUALITY ENGEL CURVES

Rank	Product group code	Product group	Slope	Standard error
1	6012	Medications/remedies/health aids	–0.2969	0.4656
2	2509	Yeast	–0.1573	0.1514
3	8808	Children's cologne & gift sets	–0.1152	0.1311
4	8803	Meal starters	–0.0915	0.0776
5	5520	Shoe care	–0.0594	0.1147
6	6009	Fragrances—women	–0.0436	0.0677
7	2508	Snacks, spreads, dips—dairy	–0.0404	0.0279
8	6006	Ethnic haba	–0.0377	0.0557
9	8806	Meal starters	–0.0247	0.0554
10	5504	Canning, freezing supplies	–0.0234	0.1329
11	6018	Vitamins	–0.0177	0.0250
12	8810	Contraceptives and pregnancy tests	–0.0136	0.1153
13	5521	Soft goods	–0.0106	0.0561
14	5518	Seasonal	–0.0077	0.1006
15	2004	Ice	–0.0014	0.0361
16	8809	Miscellaneous medical products	0.0095	0.0242
17	1009	Flour	0.0108	0.0166
18	5509	Glassware, tableware	0.0305	0.0428
19	6011	Hair care	0.0307	0.0221
20	5515	Kitchen gadgets	0.0315	0.0306
21	1508	Soft drinks—non-carbonated	0.0402	0.0632
22	1501	Bread and baked goods	0.0406	0.0105
23	2005	Ice cream, novelties	0.0422	0.0101
24	6004	Deodorant	0.0424	0.0163
25	1013	Pasta	0.0457	0.0169
26	2503	Cottage cheese, sour cream, toppings	0.0475	0.0129
27	5003	Wine	0.0478	0.0259
28	4502	Disposable diapers	0.0498	0.0385
29	8802	Fruit- and vegetable-based beverages	0.0499	0.0120
30	2001	Baked goods—frozen	0.0502	0.0167
31	1005	Cereal	0.0506	0.0096

(continued on next page)

(*Table 3-1, continued*)

Rank	Product group code	Product group	Slope	Standard error
32	2501	Butter and margarine	0.0508	0.0142
33	8805	Frozen novelties	0.0525	0.0215
34	6017	Skin care preparations	0.0544	0.0299
35	4509	Pet care	0.0552	0.0312
36	513	Soup	0.0555	0.0166
37	1006	Coffee	0.0565	0.0188
38	1020	Tea	0.0628	0.0222
39	1007	Condiments, gravies, and sauces	0.0629	0.0119
40	5002	Liquor	0.0633	0.0372
41	2507	Pudding, desserts—dairy	0.0641	0.0320
42	1016	Shortening, oil	0.0647	0.0184
43	505	Gum	0.0658	0.0296
44	2003	Desserts/fruits/toppings—frozen	0.0696	0.0249
45	6014	Oral hygiene	0.0701	0.0175
46	1018	Sugar, sweeteners	0.0714	0.0177
47	514	Vegetables—canned	0.0715	0.0151
48	6013	Men's toiletries	0.0728	0.0742
49	511	Prepared food—dry mixes	0.0729	0.0150
50	6016	Shaving needs	0.0731	0.0378
51	3001	Dressings/salads/prep foods—deli	0.0738	0.0145
52	6002	Cosmetics	0.0740	0.0298
53	506	Jams, jellies, spreads	0.0762	0.0149
54	4001	Fresh produce	0.0768	0.0106
55	6010	Grooming aids	0.0773	0.0315
56	6007	Feminine hygiene	0.0777	0.0657
57	503	Candy	0.0780	0.0157
58	512	Seafood—canned	0.0783	0.0279
59	1014	Pickles, olives, and relish	0.0797	0.0160
60	2505	Eggs	0.0814	0.0097
61	5506	Cookware	0.0819	0.0502
62	504	Fruit—canned	0.0822	0.0140
63	4505	Household supplies	0.0850	0.0263
64	1506	Crackers	0.0853	0.0121
65	2502	Cheese	0.0861	0.0117

(*continued on next page*)

(Table 3-1, continued)

Rank	Product group code	Product group	Slope	Standard error
66	510	Prepared food—ready-to-serve	0.0862	0.0195
67	5519	Sewing notions	0.0879	0.0694
68	5510	Greeting cards/party needs/novelties	0.0901	0.0519
69	1019	Table syrups, molasses	0.0903	0.0202
70	5503	Books and magazines	0.0910	0.0467
71	2506	Milk	0.0932	0.0083
72	5511	Hardware, tools	0.0943	0.0345
73	1004	Breakfast food	0.0944	0.0192
74	5514	Insecticides/pesticides/rodenticides	0.0952	0.0434
75	1002	Baking supplies	0.0977	0.0128
76	1015	Salad dressings, mayo, toppings	0.0983	0.0122
77	4503	Fresheners and deodorizers	0.0985	0.0248
78	2504	Dough products	0.0995	0.0186
79	6015	Sanitary protection	0.0999	0.0227
80	1503	Carbonated beverages	0.1009	0.0174
81	3002	Packaged meats—deli	0.1014	0.0125
82	8811	Pain remedies	0.1023	0.0249
83	2010	Vegetables—frozen	0.1025	0.0133
84	2007	Pizza/snacks/hors d'oeuvres—frzn	0.1025	0.0214
85	1011	Nuts	0.1046	0.0205
86	6008	First aid	0.1052	0.0320
87	8807	Wine-flavored refreshment and coolers	0.1090	0.0773
88	5522	Stationery, school supplies	0.1092	0.0234
89	2002	Breakfast foods—frozen	0.1101	0.0208
90	4504	Household cleaners	0.1113	0.0185
91	2006	Juices, drinks—frozen	0.1124	0.0321
92	8801	Non-alcoholic non-carbonated beverages	0.1127	0.0148
93	1001	Baking mixes	0.1144	0.0208
94	1012	Packaged milk and modifiers	0.1160	0.0199
95	1010	Fruit—dried	0.1180	0.0206
96	1505	Cookies	0.1190	0.0150
97	2009	Unprep meat/poultry/seafood—frzn	0.1217	0.0244

(continued on next page)

(Table 3-1, continued)

Rank	Product group code	Product group	Slope	Standard error
98	1507	Snacks	0.1224	0.0132
99	5001	Beer	0.1228	0.0382
100	1017	Spices, seasoning, extracts	0.1262	0.0206
101	3501	Fresh meat	0.1301	0.0325
102	6003	Cough and cold remedies	0.1311	0.0235
103	5501	Automotive	0.1324	0.0430
104	508	Pet food	0.1324	0.0377
105	5507	Electronics, records, tapes	0.1366	0.0264
106	5516	Light bulbs, electric goods	0.1369	0.0360
107	5508	Floral, gardening	0.1380	0.1114
108	4506	Laundry supplies	0.1408	0.0201
109	6001	Baby needs	0.1411	0.0585
110	4511	Wrapping materials and bags	0.1429	0.0176
111	4507	Paper products	0.1431	0.0170
112	1021	Vegetables and grains—dried	0.1460	0.0266
113	501	Baby food	0.1482	0.0973
114	5512	Hosiery, socks	0.1500	0.0767
115	4508	Personal soap and bath additives	0.1503	0.0206
116	8804	Bottled beverages	0.1513	0.0304
117	2510	Yogurt	0.1531	0.0260
118	1008	Desserts, gelatins, syrup	0.1536	0.0223
119	2008	Prepared foods—frozen	0.1562	0.0193
120	5517	Photographic supplies	0.1582	0.0518
121	5513	Housewares, appliances	0.1613	0.0412
122	8812	Meal starters	0.1672	0.1665
123	6005	Diet aids	0.1840	0.0786
124	4501	Detergents	0.1862	0.0179
125	5502	Batteries and flashlights	0.2058	0.0238
126	4510	Tobacco & accessories	0.2582	0.0585
127	5505	Charcoal, logs, accessories	0.2626	0.0807
128	5524	Toys & sporting goods	0.3228	0.0771

SOURCE: Authors' regressions and ACNielsen Homescan.
NOTE: The slope β of the quality Engel curve is estimated from the following regression: $uv_{gh} = \alpha + \beta_g y_{gh} + \varepsilon_{gh}$, where uv_{gh} is the log unit value of goods in product group g purchased by household h, y_{gh} is log expenditure per adult of household h, and ε_{gh} is an error term.

FIGURE 3-1

ESTIMATED QUALITY ENGEL CURVES FOR SELECTED PRODUCTS

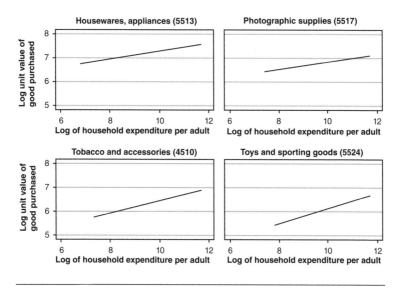

SOURCE: Table 3-1.
NOTE: See the text for a description of the Engel curve regressions.

that wealthier households do tend to buy higher-quality varieties of a wide range of goods. In 70 percent of cases there is a statistically significant positive relationship between the average price paid within a product group for an item and household expenditure per adult. Figure 3-1 plots this relationship for some of the categories with steeper upward slopes. For example, a 1 percent increase in expenditure is associated with a 0.26 percent increase in expenditure on tobacco products, and a 0.32 percent increase in the price paid for toys and sporting goods. Figure 3-2 plots the slopes of each of the 128 goods against the ratio of expenditure on that good by households in the highest tercile to that in the lowest. Interestingly, the rich spend relatively more on goods with a steeper quality slope.

Richer households do not just tend to buy more-expensive products than poorer households; they also consume a wider range of

FIGURE 3-2

REGRESSION OF RELATIVE EXPENDITURE SHARES ON
ESTIMATED COEFFICIENTS OF QUALITY ENGEL CURVES

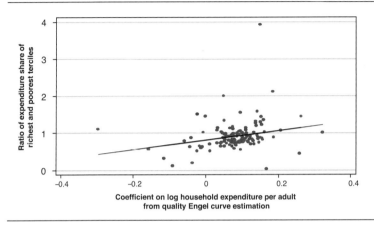

SOURCE: Authors' regressions.
NOTES: Each observation represents one of the 128 product groups listed in table 3-1. The slope of the regression is 1.687 and is significant at the 1 percent level. The R^2 of the regression is 0.28. Quality Engel curve slopes calculated using per adult household consumption as a measure of household income.

products. To confirm this we regressed the logarithm of the number of different products purchased by households on the log of expenditure per adult and the number of members in the household. (The latter variable is included to control for the fact that larger households have more members and therefore more diverse tastes.) The results, presented in table 3-2, indicate a very strong tendency for wealthier households to consume a wider variety of goods: a 1 percent increase in household expenditure is associated with a 34 percent increase in the number of products purchased within a product category. Taken together, these results indicate that as households become wealthier, they systematically expand the set of goods they consume and gradually shift their consumption toward more expensive varieties of goods.

A systematic way of describing the different patterns of consumption of rich and poor is to decompose the consumption expenditures

TABLE 3-2

ESTIMATED VARIETY ENGEL CURVES

Rank	Product group code	Product group	Slope	Standard error
1	8812	Meal starters	0.1998	0.0551
2	2004	Ice	0.2701	0.0273
3	5524	Toys & sporting goods	0.2812	0.0136
4	2006	Juices, drinks—frozen	0.2924	0.0132
5	1009	Flour	0.2941	0.0070
6	5506	Cookware	0.2973	0.0103
7	6013	Men's toiletries	0.3003	0.0213
8	504	Fruit—canned	0.3029	0.0062
9	5521	Soft goods	0.3037	0.0172
10	2003	Desserts/fruits/toppings—frozen	0.3045	0.0079
11	6007	Feminine hygiene	0.3066	0.0171
12	2504	Dough products	0.3067	0.0068
13	1008	Desserts, gelatins, syrup	0.3088	0.0065
14	3501	Fresh meat	0.3095	0.0107
15	1508	Soft drinks—non-carbonated	0.3096	0.0117
16	5510	Greeting cards/party needs/novelties	0.3101	0.0119
17	2507	Pudding, desserts—dairy	0.3108	0.0150
18	1001	Baking mixes	0.3109	0.0061
19	1019	Table syrups, molasses	0.3110	0.0084
20	1018	Sugar, sweeteners	0.3113	0.0064
21	1010	Fruit—dried	0.3114	0.0087
22	5512	Hosiery, socks	0.3116	0.0196
23	2001	Baked goods—frozen	0.3124	0.0069
24	1002	Baking supplies	0.3125	0.0059
25	1016	Shortening, oil	0.3128	0.0069
26	1017	Spices, seasoning, extracts	0.3136	0.0063
27	6005	Diet aids	0.3151	0.0206
28	2503	Cot cheese, sour cream, toppings	0.3153	0.0064
29	1014	Pickles, olives, and relish	0.3157	0.0069
30	8806	Meal starters	0.3165	0.0303
31	2509	Yeast	0.3194	0.0932
32	2009	Unprep meat/poultry/seafood—frzn	0.3194	0.0078

(continued on next page)

(Table 3-2, continued)

Rank	Product group code	Product group	Slope	Standard error
33	5515	Kitchen gadgets	0.3196	0.0078
34	1021	Vegetables and grains—dried	0.3202	0.0084
35	6012	Medications/remedies/health aids	0.3217	0.0611
36	1012	Packaged milk and modifiers	0.3218	0.0068
37	5501	Automotive	0.3232	0.0122
38	2501	Butter and margarine	0.3236	0.0059
39	4508	Personal soap and bath additives	0.3240	0.0071
40	5518	Seasonal	0.3254	0.0260
41	6009	Fragrances—women	0.3254	0.0139
42	4511	Wrapping materials and bags	0.3256	0.0064
43	5505	Charcoal, logs, accessories	0.3259	0.0193
44	8811	Pain remedies	0.3263	0.0091
45	512	Seafood—canned	0.3273	0.0078
46	2508	Snacks, spreads, dips—dairy	0.3274	0.0101
47	6008	First aid	0.3279	0.0084
48	1015	Salad dressings, mayo, toppings	0.3281	0.0064
49	2005	Ice cream, novelties	0.3290	0.0072
50	5504	Canning, freezing supplies	0.3294	0.0322
51	8807	Wine-flavored refreshment and coolers	0.3306	0.0200
52	2002	Breakfast foods—frozen	0.3306	0.0087
53	2505	Eggs	0.3311	0.0058
54	1506	Crackers	0.3313	0.0063
55	505	Gum	0.3314	0.0088
56	514	Vegetables—canned	0.3317	0.0059
57	1013	Pasta	0.3321	0.0065
58	1011	Nuts	0.3337	0.0070
59	4509	Pet care	0.3340	0.0094
60	2010	Vegetables—frozen	0.3343	0.0065
61	6006	Ethnic haba	0.3347	0.0244
62	4506	Laundry supplies	0.3361	0.0069
63	506	Jams, jellies, spreads	0.3364	0.0073
64	5522	Stationery, school supplies	0.3370	0.0071
65	2502	Cheese	0.3374	0.0058
66	1006	Coffee	0.3376	0.0075

(continued on next page)

(Table 3-2, continued)

Rank	Product group code	Product group	Slope	Standard error
67	8805	Frozen novelties	0.3381	0.0095
68	511	Prepared food—dry mixes	0.3382	0.0060
69	4503	Fresheners and deodorizers	0.3387	0.0084
70	5517	Photographic supplies	0.3390	0.0120
71	510	Prepared food—ready-to-serve	0.3392	0.0067
72	6010	Grooming aids	0.3394	0.0088
73	6015	Sanitary protection	0.3397	0.0084
74	2007	Pizza/snacks/hors d'oeuvres—frzn	0.3401	0.0078
75	1007	Condiments, gravies, and sauces	0.3403	0.0060
76	5003	Wine	0.3404	0.0112
77	5509	Glassware, tableware	0.3404	0.0094
78	5520	Shoe care	0.3405	0.0385
79	5502	Batteries and flashlights	0.3407	0.0077
80	1004	Breakfast food	0.3408	0.0083
81	6011	Hair care	0.3423	0.0068
82	3002	Packaged meats—deli	0.3429	0.0059
83	6014	Oral hygiene	0.3432	0.0070
84	513	Soup	0.3436	0.0061
85	6003	Cough and cold remedies	0.3437	0.0081
86	5508	Floral, gardening	0.3438	0.0234
87	4502	Disposable diapers	0.3440	0.0161
88	3001	Dressings/salads/prep foods—deli	0.3442	0.0065
89	2510	Yogurt	0.3443	0.0076
90	1505	Cookies	0.3446	0.0065
91	5519	Sewing notions	0.3451	0.0143
92	4504	Household cleaners	0.3470	0.0071
93	6001	Baby needs	0.3470	0.0137
94	2008	Prepared foods—frozen	0.3474	0.0066
95	4001	Fresh produce	0.3481	0.0059
96	4501	Detergents	0.3482	0.0063
97	6018	Vitamins	0.3485	0.0088
98	5516	Light bulbs, electric goods	0.3489	0.0083
99	4505	Household supplies	0.3491	0.0074
100	6016	Shaving needs	0.3494	0.0106

(continued on next page)

(*Table 3-2, continued*)

Rank	Product group code	Product group	Slope	Standard error
101	1503	Carbonated beverages	0.3524	0.0062
102	1020	Tea	0.3527	0.0088
103	4510	Tobacco & accessories	0.3546	0.0138
104	4507	Paper products	0.3560	0.0060
105	501	Baby food	0.3564	0.0182
106	6017	Skin care preparations	0.3568	0.0089
107	8801	Non-alcoholic non-carbonated beverages	0.3585	0.0064
108	8809	Miscellaneous medical products	0.3603	0.0073
109	8804	Bottled beverages	0.3607	0.0082
110	6004	Deodorant	0.3620	0.0081
111	503	Candy	0.3620	0.0063
112	8802	Fruit- and vegetable-based beverages	0.3623	0.0071
113	5513	Housewares, appliances	0.3628	0.0088
114	1005	Cereal	0.3631	0.0066
115	5511	Hardware, tools	0.3632	0.0095
116	1501	Bread and baked goods	0.3635	0.0060
117	508	Pet food	0.3642	0.0081
118	5002	Liquor	0.3656	0.0135
119	1507	Snacks	0.3669	0.0062
120	2506	Milk	0.3673	0.0061
121	5001	Beer	0.3681	0.0128
122	5503	Books and magazines	0.3703	0.0159
123	5514	Insecticides/pesticides/rodenticides	0.3713	0.0156
124	5507	Electronics, records, tapes	0.3725	0.0084
125	8810	Contraceptives and pregnancy tests	0.3786	0.0412
126	6002	Cosmetics	0.3905	0.0092
127	8803	Meal starters	0.5213	0.1418
128	8808	Children's cologne & gift sets	0.6079	0.0561

SOURCE: Authors' regressions and ACNielsen Homescan.

NOTE: The slope β of the variety Engel curve is estimated from the following regression: $v_{gh} = \cdot\alpha + \beta_1 y_{gh} + \beta_2 Size_h + \varepsilon_{gh}$, where v_{gh} is the log of the number of different UPC codes in product group g purchased by household h, $Size_h$ is the number of members in household h, y_{gh} is the of log of expenditure per adult of household h, and ε_{gh} is an error term.

of different income groups into "intensive" and "extensive" margins. For this purpose we adapt Feenstra's (1994) methodology in a way similar to that of Hummels and Klenow (2005). The intensive margin captures extra expenditure by a particular household group on goods that other household groups also purchase, and the extensive margin captures expenditure on different goods. For example, if wealthy households buy more of the same milk than poorer households, this difference is captured in the intensive margin, but if they purchase different types of milk (for example, organic), that difference is captured in the extensive margin. Using this methodology, we can further decompose the intensive margin into differences in the price paid and the quantity consumed by income groups.

We begin by explaining our measure of the extensive margin. The extensive margin index EM_h captures the similarity in consumption baskets between household h and a reference household $\sim h$. It is defined as follows:

$$3) \quad EM_h = \frac{\sum_{u \in I_h} p_{um\sim h} x_{um\sim h}}{\sum_{u \in I} p_{um\sim h} x_{um\sim h}}$$

where u are UPCs, m are modules (product groups), I_h is the set of UPCs for which household h has positive consumption, and I is the set of all UPCs. The numerator of the ratio in equation 3 is the sum of expenditures (price p times quantity x) by other households only on the items purchased by household h. The denominator covers all expenditures by the set of other households. If all households consume the same set of goods, EM_h will equal one, but if household h does not purchase all the UPCs in all modules, this measure will be less than one. The extensive margin can be thought of as a weighted count of categories purchased by household h relative to the set of categories purchased by all other households. If all categories are of equal importance, then the extensive margin is simply the fraction of all UPCs purchased by consumers in category h. The main deviation from this intuition is that categories are weighted by their importance in the consumption of other households.

A simple example will help demonstrate the significance of this measure. If expenditure per UPC is constant across all UPCs, and the typical low-income household consumes products in only one-third of the UPCs that the typical household consumes, this implies that $EM_h = 1/3$. The lower the index, the fewer UPCs this group of households consumes relative to the typical household. A full description of this measure can be found in Hummels and Klenow (2005).

The corresponding intensive margin IM_h compares expenditure by h and $\sim h$ on a common set of goods. It is given by

$$4) \qquad IM_h = \frac{\sum_{u \in I_h} p_{umh} x_{umh}}{\sum_{u \in I_h} p_{um\sim h} x_{um\sim h}}$$

In other words, IM_h equals h's nominal consumption relative to the nominal consumption of other households *in the same categories that h consumes*. It thus examines how much less the poor consume relative to the rich in the UPCs purchased by the poor. For example, if the poor consume half as many UPCs as the rich, and all categories are of equal importance, IM_h for the poor will be 1/2.

We can now put these two indexes together, and decompose aggregate consumption as follows:

$$5) \qquad \frac{Exp_h}{Exp_{\sim h}} = \frac{\sum_{u \in I_h} p_{umh} x_{umh}}{\sum_{u \in I_h} p_{um\sim h} x_{um\sim h}} = \frac{\sum_{u \in I_h} p_{um\sim h} x_{um\sim h}}{\sum_{u \in I_h} p_{um\sim h} x_{um\sim h}} \times \frac{\sum_{u \in I_h} p_{umh} x_{umh}}{\sum_{u \in I_h} p_{um\sim h} x_{um\sim h}}$$

$$= EM_h \times IM_h$$

where Exp_h is total expenditure of household h as a share of overall expenditure. This equation is an analogue of Feenstra's new varieties adjustment to an import price index, but applied to a cross section of households. The left-hand side of the equation measures how much more or less household h consumes relative to household $\sim h$. In our empirical specification, household h will represent the typical low-income household in the United States, and $\sim h$ all other U.S. households. The difference in consumption between the poor households and the middle- and high-income households can be decomposed into the extensive margin and the intensive margin.

As a simple example of the intensive versus extensive decomposition,

TABLE 3-3

DECOMPOSITION OF DIFFERENCES IN CONSUMPTION AND PRICES
PAID BETWEEN LOW-INCOME AND OTHER HOUSEHOLDS

Household group	Difference in total consumption[a] (percent)	Sources of difference in total consumption (percent)	
		Extensive margin[b]	Intensive margin[c]
Middle income	34.6	17.5	82.5
High income	74.1	19.7	80.3

SOURCE: Authors' calculations.

NOTES: a. Average amount by which consumption by the indicated income group exceeds that of low-income households; b. share of total difference resulting from consumption by the indicated household group of goods not consumed by low-income households; c. share of total difference resulting from consumption by the indicated household group of goods also consumed

we compare the consumption expenditure of the lowest tercile of the income distribution with that of the highest tercile. It is not surprising that the highest tercile consumes 74 percent more than the lowest. The interesting question that this decomposition can address is *what* the rich consume more *of* than the poor. Some of this additional consumption comes from a greater number of UPCs consumed: the rich consume 15 percent more UPCs than the poor. As a result, roughly 20 percent of their higher consumption comes from purchases of additional varieties, and the rest from greater consumption of the same UPCs. Middle-income households display a similar pattern: for every dollar of additional expenditure, they spend about 82 cents on products also purchased by the poor and 18 cents on different goods. Thus we observe a similar pattern in which wealthier households do not just consume more of everything, but also consume goods that poor households do not—that is, the rich consume a greater variety. These patterns are detailed in table 3-3.

We can also decompose differences in the prices paid by different income groups into two components: differences in prices of goods that they both consume, and higher prices for product categories, which we refer to as "modules."[1] We refer to the former as the "shopping effect," because it captures factors, such as nicer

Difference in prices paid[d] (percent)	Sources of difference in prices paid (percentage)	
	"Quality" effect[e]	"Shopping" effect[f]
11.9	87.6	12.4
32.9	84.4	15.6

by low-income households; d. average amount by which prices paid by the indicated household group exceed those paid by low-income households; e. share of total difference resulting from higher quality of goods purchased by the indicated household group, or more pleasant shopping experience, than by low-income households; f. share of total difference resulting from difference in prices paid by household groups for the same goods.

stores or less attention to price, that might cause wealthier households to spend more for the same goods. We refer to the latter term as the "quality effect," because it captures the fact that wealthier households tend to purchase more expensive varieties of particular product groups.

Formally, we can define the exact price index between two income groups h and k as

6) $$P_h = \prod_{m \in M} \left(\frac{p_{mh}}{p_{mk}} \right)$$

where $m \in M$ is a particular module m that belongs to the set of all available modules M, $P_{mh} = \prod_{u \in I_h}(P_{umh})^{W_{umh}} = \prod_{u \in I_c}(P_{umh})^{W_{umh}} \times \prod_{\substack{u \in I_h \\ u \notin I_c}}(P_{umh})^{W_{umh}} = P_{mh}^{Common} \times P_{mh}^{Non-Common}$ and $\sum_{u \in I_{mh}} w_{umh} = w_{mh}$. This implies that equation 6 can be divided into two components:

7) $$P_h = \underbrace{\frac{P_{mh}^{Common}}{P_{mk}^{Common}}}_{\text{"Shopping" Effect}} \times \underbrace{\frac{P_{mh}^{Non-Common}}{P_{mk}^{Non-Common}}}_{\text{"Quality" Effect}}$$

This decomposition reveals several important facts about how prices vary for consumers of different incomes. First, the prices paid per module by middle-income and rich households are on average 12 and 33 percent higher, respectively, than the prices paid by poor households. For instance, rich households pay 33 percent higher prices for products that belong to the module "baby milk." Between 85 and 90 percent of this difference arises from the fact that the poor tend to purchase lower-priced UPCs within this module (see the column "Quality" in table 3-3). The remaining difference arises because poor households manage to find the same UPCs that the rich purchase but pay less for them (see the column "Shopping" in table 3-3).

One important implication is that gaps between the wealthy and the poor are smaller than one might think based on data using a common price index. Obviously some of the difference in the prices paid by wealthy and poor people pays for nicer shopping experiences for the rich, for example in boutiques rather than outlet malls, or less time spent shopping. However, probably an important part of the difference arises from truly lower prices for the same goods in areas where poor people shop. To the extent that this is a true price differential, we can estimate its magnitude. Since the wealthy pay 33 percent more for their goods than the poor, and 16 percent of this difference is due to price differences paid for the same goods, we can estimate that the poor have as much as 5 percent (0.33 x 0.16) more real expenditure relative to the rich because of their lower price index.

In other words, if the poor can access the same goods as the rich at a lower price, the use of "common" price indexes between income groups misses an important difference in the relative real incomes of poor and rich households. Inequality measures that are based on a common price index ignore this effect. If we believe that the lower price paid by the poor is a pure income gain, then the ratio of the real income of the 90th-percentile household to that of the 10th-percentile household is not 4.49 (as estimated in CBO 2006) but actually 4.26, or 5 percent smaller (see table 3-4). Under the assumption that only 50 percent of the lower prices paid by the poor implies higher real income (and the other half reflects extra

TABLE 3-4
ADJUSTMENTS TO INEQUALITY MEASURE FOR
DIFFERENCES IN PRICES PAID, 1994–2005

Measure	1994	2000	2005
90–10 income ratio, conventional measure	4.43	4.33	4.49
90–10 income ratio adjusted for:			
100% of "shopping" effect[a]	4.21	4.11	4.26
50% of "shopping" effect	4.32	4.22	4.38
Difference in 90–10 ratio relative to 2005 (percent)			
Assuming identical consumption baskets	1.4	3.7	
Assuming different consumption baskets	3.6	4.7	

SOURCE: Congressional Budget Office (2006) and authors' calculations.
NOTE: a. See table 3-3 for definition.

time shopping or a less pleasant shopping experience), the real wage of the 90th-percentile household is 4.38 times that of the 10th-percentile household, which means that inequality is 2.5 percent less than suggested by national statistics.

China and the Poor in America

We now are in a position to examine one dimension of how international trade has been affecting the consumption prices of the poor. The full impact of international trade on wages is a vast and complex topic that goes far beyond the scope of this monograph. However, we can address one part of the topic that has not been the focus of much discussion: how does the entry of China into U.S. markets affect the relative prices paid by wealthy and poor households?[2]

We have already discussed the important role that China has played in the growing number of new goods entering the United States. Nearly two-thirds of all U.S. import markets have at least one Chinese firm operating in them. How this affects consumers is more subtle. To assess this impact, we first matched the ten-digit HS categories of the trade data with the ACNielsen modules. This matching allows us to examine the relationship between prices in U.S. retail stores and the increased market participation of Chinese imports. We computed the value of imports from China as a share of total U.S. imports in each of these modules. Between 1994 and 2003, the average change in the Chinese share of imports was 6 percentage points. However, there is a lot of dispersion in Chinese import penetration. If we rank modules by the change in China's import share, we find that at the 10th percentile the change in China's share was zero, but it was 23 percent at the 90th percentile.

To assess what impact this had on prices, we regressed the log change in each module's price index (adjusted for new goods) on the corresponding share of Chinese exports. Overall, sectors in which China's market share rose faster exhibited price declines relative to sectors with less Chinese import penetration: a 1 percent increase in Chinese market share is associated with a 0.2 percent decline in the price of goods common to the sector over the entire period, and a 0.3 percent decline in a price index adjusted for the increased number and quality of goods. These numbers, of course, cannot be interpreted as the net gain to the United States from greater import competition from China, because they do not include the impact on factor prices (most importantly, wages) or on export prices, but they suggest that China exerts an important competitive effect on U.S. industries.

We can also get a sense of the differential impact of China on the consumption baskets of rich and poor households, because these households allocate different shares of their expenditure to goods that China produces. The two lower panels of table 3-5 show that a 1-percentage-point increase in the share of Chinese imports is associated with a statistically significant 0.15-percentage-point fall in prices of common goods for low-income households (defined as the lowest decile of the income distribution) but with half as large (and not statistically significant) a drop in the prices of goods purchased by the rich. This difference is driven by the fact that poor households purchase relatively more goods that are sourced in China than the rich. The impacts are even larger when variety-adjusted price

TABLE 3-5

IMPACT OF CHINESE IMPORTS ON U.S. RETAIL PRICES
BY INCOME GROUP

	Median module log price change	Log change in price index (common goods)	Log change in price index (all goods)
Overall U.S. consumption basket			
Change in Chinese import	–0.064	–0.089	–0.296
share, 1994–2003	0.96	(1.99)*	(4.67)**
Constant	0.154	0.106	–0.003
	(3.87)**	(2.54)*	–0.06
No. of observations	434	433	493
R^2	0	0	0.03
Basket of goods consumed by the poor			
Change in Chinese import	–0.198	–0.146	–0.312
share, 1994–2003	(2.17)*	(2.93)**	(4.64)**
Constant	0.204	0.111	–0.294
	(2.74)**	(2.35)*	(6.28)**
No. of observations	368	368	456
R^2	0.01	0.02	0.06
Basket of goods consumed by the rich			
Change in Chinese import	–0.082	–0.07	–0.197
share, 1994–2003	(–1.23)	(–1.53)	(2.72)**
Constant	0.169	0.08	–0.335
	(3.83)**	(2.30)*	(7.25)**
No. of observations	356	356	446
R^2	0	0.01	0.02
Difference in estimated coefficients between poor and rich	–0.116	–0.076	–0.115

SOURCE: Authors' regressions and ACNielsen Homescan.
NOTE: Robust t-statistics are in parentheses. Asterisks indicate statistical significance at the *5 percent and the **1 percent level.

indexes are used: a 1-percentage-point increase in the share of imports from China is now associated with a 0.3-percentage-point drop in prices paid by the poor and a 0.2-percentage-point drop in prices paid by wealthy households. These findings indicate that the entry of China into U.S. markets generates a somewhat larger price decline for poorer households, perhaps driven by the fact that poorer households are more likely to consume the low-end manufactures produced in China.

In sum, we find that in modules where the Chinese presence increased substantially (those in the 90th percentile of import increases), prices fell more than 8 percent faster than in those without a Chinese presence. Given that in the typical sector the average share of Chinese imports rose by 6 percentage points, the expansion of imports from China drove down the prices paid by poor families by 0.6 percent more than the prices paid by wealthy households. Although this is admittedly not a large impact, the increased presence of Chinese products in consumer markets is associated with relatively larger gains for poor households than for rich households.

Conclusion

The results of this monograph suggest that product innovation and consumer behavior are important factors in understanding both the level of and changes in poverty and inequality in the United States. We identify two important channels through which these factors have an effect. First, official definitions of the poverty line are significantly biased upward, because the CPI-U, on which the poverty line is based, does not take into account new goods and the ability of poor people to substitute away from expensive goods and toward cheaper goods over time. Accounting for this first effect leads to a poverty rate that is probably less than half as high as is conventionally believed. Second, the fact that poorer people pay less for the same items than do richer people means that their real incomes are higher than what conventional measures, which assume that they pay the same price, suggest. To the extent that this represents lower prices in poor neighborhoods that are not related to the amount of time people spend shopping or the quality of their shopping experience, this constitutes a real income gain and should be reflected in a lower measured level of inequality. Similarly, Chinese imports seem to benefit poor U.S. consumers by driving down the prices of goods they tend to consume disproportionately.

The bottom line is that if one defines poverty according to a cost-of-living standard, U.S. economic growth has dramatically reduced the share of Americans living in poverty. The same analysis we have applied to the poverty line applies equally to Americans in other income classes; all Americans are substantially better off economically than they were a quarter century ago.

Notes

Introduction

1. CBO (2006). See also Webster and Bishaw (2006).

2. For a detailed examination of the quality and new goods bias, see Broda and Weinstein (2008). For a summary of the impact of CPI biases on other important economic indicators, see Broda (2004).

3. On the impact of new imported products on the U.S. import price index, see Broda and Weinstein (2004, 2006, 2007).

4. These results are based on current work in progress by Broda and Romalis (2008).

Chapter 1: Explaining CPI Biases

1. Until 1998 the CPI used expenditure data from 1982 to 1984 to construct the market basket of goods and services. In 1998 the base period was revised to 1993–95, which is still used at present.

2. A simple example can illustrate the magnitude of the bias. Assume that the typical household buys five bottles of Coke and five bottles of Pepsi a month at a cost of one dollar per bottle. If the price of Coke doubles to two dollars and the price of Pepsi falls to 50 cents, most consumers will switch their purchases toward Pepsi, and thus may keep their total spending on soda the same as before (or less, if they switch entirely to Pepsi). But a fixed-quantity index like the CPI-U will record this set of price changes as a 25 percent increase in the price of soda, because the total cost of five bottles each of Coke and Pepsi has risen from $10 to $12.50. That is, the CPI methodology assumes that consumers continue to buy the same amount of Coke and Pepsi even after their prices change, and thus the price change contributes to a rise in measured inflation.

3. Current statistical procedures do not do a very good job of identifying, measuring, and estimating the value and the pricing of new products as they enter the economy. The BLS's approach is to omit the introduction of new

goods in its calculation of the CPI until they are eventually discovered as part of the gradual rotation of the sample of goods. Even when the no-longer-new good eventually enters the CPI calculation, no adjustment is made for the consumer gains it provides in relation to the earlier goods.

4. For a discussion of the problems underlying price index theory, see Diewert (1993).

5. The use of scanner data to compute price indexes has large benefits relative to official statistics. For more applications see Feenstra and Shapiro (2003).

6. The BLS substitutes goods of comparable quality when a good disappears from the market, but this solves the problem only if the two goods are identical from consumers' perspective, which is generally not the case.

7. The conventional growth rate can be written as $2g/(2 - g)$.

8. The results in this section heavily rely on Broda and Weinstein (2006).

9. The existing literature has defined varieties in a number of ways. One option is to define varieties as goods coming from a particular firm. This encounters the problem that not all goods from a given firm are of the same variety. More practically, it is very difficult to get firm- or plant-level data for a large set of countries that export to the United States. Whether consumers assess goods coming from different countries as different "varieties" is something we will be able to measure by estimating consumers' willingness to substitute among these varieties. If consumers find coffee from Brazil to be very similar to that of Colombia, we should find high levels of substitutability between the two.

10. Technically, the 2001 category contains only nondecaffeinated coffee in packages of under 2 kilograms. The actual number of suppliers could be higher.

11. As the name suggests, a fixed-weight index adds prices of different goods and services using weights for each good or service that are fixed over time. Both the CPI-U and the import price index are fixed-weight indexes.

Chapter 3: Prices and Inequality, 1990–2005

1. Modules are disaggregate product categories, like milk and coffee. A good's unit value is its price per unit of quantity, for instance, the price per ounce of a particular type of milk. Typically organic milk has a higher unit value than regular milk.

2. This section relies on work in progress by Broda and Romalis (2008).

References

Advisory Commission to Study the Consumer Price Index. 1996. "Toward a More Accurate Measure of the Cost of Living." Final report to the Senate Finance Committee. Washington, D.C. www.ssa.gov/history/reports/boskinrpt.html.

Bils, Mark, and Peter J. Klenow. 2001. "Quantifying Quality Growth." *American Economic Review* 91(4): 1006–30.

Broda, Christian. 2004. "Consumer Price Index Biases and Their Impact on Policy." *International Perspectives* 32. New York: International Research Department, Federal Reserve Bank of New York (July).

Broda, Christian, and David E. Weinstein. 2004. "Variety Growth and World Welfare." *American Economic Review* 94(2): 139–44.

_____. 2006. "Globalization and the Gains from Variety." *Quarterly Journal of Economics* 121(2): 541–85.

_____.2007. "Defining Price Stability in Japan: A View from America." Working Paper 13255. Cambridge, Mass.: National Bureau of Economic Research (July).

_____. 2008. "Product Creation and Destruction: Evidence and Price Implications." *American Economic Review* (forthcoming).

Broda, Christian, and John Romalis. 2008. "Inequality and Prices: Does China Benefit the Poor in America?" Chicago: University of Chicago Graduate School of Business.

Congressional Budget Office (CBO). 2006. "Changes in the Low-Wage Labor Markets between 1979 and 2005." Publication 2745. Washington, D.C. (December).

Costa, D. 2001. "Estimating Real Income in the United States from 1888 to 1994: Correcting CPI Bias Using Engel Curves." *Journal of Political Economy* 109(6): 1288–1310.

Davis, Steve, and J. Haltiwanger. 1992. "Gross Job Creation, Gross Job Destruction, and Employment Reallocation." *Quarterly Journal of Economics* 107(3): 819–63.

Diewert, W. Erwin. 1993. "The Early History of Price Index Research." In *Essays in Index Number Theory*, Vol. 1, ed. W. E. Diewert and A. O. Nakamura. Amsterdam: Elsevier Science Publishers.

Feenstra, R. 1994. "New Product Varieties and the Measurement of International Prices." *American Economic Review* 84(1): 157–77.

Feenstra, R., and M. Shapiro. 2003. *Scanner Data and Price Indexes*. Studies of Income and Wealth, vol. 64. Chicago: University of Chicago Press.

Feenstra, Robert C., John Romalis, and Peter K. Schott. 2002. "U.S. Imports, Exports, and Tariff Data." Working Paper 9387. Cambridge, Mass.: National Bureau of Economic Research. http://cid.econ.ucdavis.edu/usixd/wp5515d.html.

Hamilton, B. 2001. "Using Engel's Law to Estimate CPI Bias." *American Economic Review* 91(3): 619–30.

Hummels, D., and P. Klenow. 2005. "The Variety and Quality of a Nation's Exports." *American Economic Review* 95(3): 704–23.

Lebow, David E., and Jeremy B. Rudd. 2003. "Measurement Error in the Consumer Price Index: Where Do We Stand?" *Journal of Economic Literature* 41: 159–201.

Webster, Bruce, Jr., and Alemayehu Bishaw. 2006. "Income, Earnings, and Poverty Data from the 2005 American Community Survey." Washington, D.C.: U.S. Census Bureau (August).

About the Authors

Christian Broda is a professor of economics at the Graduate School of Business of the University of Chicago. He studies issues related to international finance and trade, and the impact of exchange rates on asset prices and financial contracts. He has applied this research in writings for publications ranging from the *American Economic Review* and the *Quarterly Journal of Economics* to the *Financial Times* and the *New York Times*. In 2006 he was named the 2006–2008 James S. Kemper Foundation Scholar. He also serves as associate editor of the *Journal of Development Economics*, a faculty fellow for the National Bureau of Economic Research, and a panel member of *Economia*, the journal of the Latin American and Caribbean Economic Association. Professor Broda earned a bachelor's degree in economics in 1997 from the Universidad de San Andrés in Argentina. Four years later, he graduated with a Ph.D. at the Massachusetts Institute of Technology. Before joining the Graduate School of Business in 2005, Professor Broda worked at the Research Department of the Federal Reserve Bank of New York.

David E. Weinstein is Carl S. Shoup Professor of the Japanese Economy at Columbia University. He is also the associate director of research at the Center for Japanese Economy and Business of the Graduate School of Business at Columbia University, research associate and director of the Japan Project at the National Bureau of Economic Research, and a member of the Council on Foreign Relations. Previously, Professor Weinstein was a senior economist at the Federal Reserve Bank of New York and a consultant to the Federal Reserve Bank of San Francisco and the Board of Governors of the

Federal Reserve. Before joining the Columbia faculty, Professor Weinstein was the Sanford R. Robertson Associate Professor of Business Administration at the School of Business Administration at the University of Michigan as well as an associate professor of economics at Harvard University. He served as a staff economist at the Council of Economic Advisers in 1989 and 1990. His teaching and research interests include international economics, macroeconomics, corporate finance, the Japanese economy, and industrial policy. Professor Weinstein earned his Ph.D. and M.A. in economics from the University of Michigan and his B.A. at Yale University. He is the recipient of numerous grants and awards including four National Science Foundation grants, an Abe Fellowship, and a Japan Foundation Fellowship.